**Big Machines At Work**

# Earthmovers

By Hal Rogers

The Child's World® Inc. ◆ Eden Prairie, Minnesota

Published by The Child's World®, Inc.
7081 W. 192 Ave.
Eden Prairie, MN 55346

Design and Production:
The Creative Spark, San Juan Capistrano, CA

Photos: © 1998 David M. Budd Photography


**Library of Congress Cataloging-in-Publication Data**

Rogers, Hal.
    Earthmovers / by Hal Rogers.
        p.  cm.
    Summary: Describes the parts of a large earthmover, how they operate, and
the work they do.
    ISBN 1-56766-652-3 (lib. bdg. : alk. paper)
    1. Earthmoving machinery Juvenile literature. [1. Earthmoving machinery.] I. Title.
TA725.R63  1999
624.1'52—dc21                                                                99-20859
                                                                                    CIP

# Contents

# On the Job

On the job, earthmovers work at a **construction site.** They move dirt from one place to another.

An earthmover has giant tires.

It can travel across rough ground.

A **blade** scoops up dirt as the machine

moves. The blade is like a shovel.

The dirt goes into a big bin. It is called a **can.** The can is full now. Some dirt spills over the side.

The earthmover scoops up dirt. It helps make the land flat. Workers cannot put up a building until the land is perfectly flat.

14

The earthmover dumps the dirt in a huge pile. Later, another machine will take the dirt away.

Sometimes an earthmover helps workers make a road. An earthmover can flatten a hill. It can also fill up a big hole.

# Climb Aboard!

Would you like to see where the driver sits?

An earthmover's driver is called an

**operator.** The operator sits inside the **cab.**

He or she uses special **levers** to make

the machine work. The driver steers the

earthmover with a steering wheel.

# Up Close

## The inside

1. The operator's seat

2. The levers

3. The steering wheel

# The outside

1. The can

2. The cab

3. The blade

# Glossary

**blade** (BLAYD)
The blade is a long metal scoop on an earthmover. It picks up dirt like a shovel.

**cab** (KAB)
A cab is the place where the grader's driver sits. It has a seat, a steering wheel, and levers.

**can** (KAN)
The can is a big bin on an earthmover. It holds dirt after the blade scoops it up.

**construction site** (kun-STRUCK-shun SITE)
A construction site is a place where workers build something. Workers make buildings at a construction site.

**levers** (LEV-erz)
The earthmover's levers are metal bars with black knobs at the ends. The operator uses them to move the machine.

**operator** (OPP-er-ay-ter)
The operator is the person who drives the earthmover. He or she also makes the machine work.